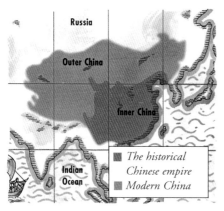

Russia

Outer China

Inner China

Indian Ocean

■ The historical Chinese empire
■ Modern China

INNER & OUTER CHINA

China is commonly divided into two areas. Inner China, the area around the basins of the Yellow and the Yangzi rivers, is the core of the historical Chinese empire, and has sustained a continuous civilization since the Stone Age. Modern or Outer China includes Manchuria, Inner Mongolia, Xinjiang and Tibet – vast areas of land that were considered by the Chinese to be foreign countries until relatively recently.

中国

THE MIDDLE KINGDOM

The Chinese name for their country is Zhong Guo (The Middle Kingdom), supposedly the centre of the world. The symbol for middle consists of a line going straight through the centre of a hole. The symbol for kingdom shows a king with a jewel, surrounded by a square to signify the borders of his kingdom.

EARLY MONEY

The bronze coin above (c. 220 BC) is circular to represent the Earth, with a square hole to represent Heaven. The symbol to the right of the hole means 'shell', since earlier in the Shang Dynasty, cowrie shells were used as money. Early Chinese states soon developed their own currencies, including bricks of tea and metal chits. During the reign of the First Emperor, coins were standardized throughout the empire.

CHINESE DYNASTIES

2100–1600 BC
Xia Dynasty (Legendary)
1600–1100 BC
Shang Dynasty (North China only)
1100–221 BC
Zhou Dynasty (North China only)

IMPERIAL CHINA

221–207 BC
Qin Dynasty
206 BC – AD 220
Han Dynasty
220–280
Three Kingdoms Period
265–420
Jin Dynasty
420–589
Southern and Northern Dynasties (including Song, Qi, Liang, Chen, North, East & West Wei, North Qi and Northern Zhou)
581–618
Sui Dynasty
618–907
Tang Dynasty
907–979
Five Dynasties and Ten Kingdoms
960–1279
Song Dynasty (North and South)
916–1125
Liao Dynasty
1115–1234
Kin Dynasty
1260–1368
Yuan Dynasty (Mongols take over)
1368–1644
Ming Dynasty
1644–1912
Qing Dynasty (Manchus take over)
1912
Last Emperor deposed

POST-IMPERIAL CHINA

1912–1949
Republic
1949–present day
People's Republic (Communist rule)

Life for the Rich

THE EXAM SYSTEM

In times of war, prowess on the battlefield could help someone rise through the ranks in society. In times of peace, the only way to advance was by becoming a civil servant. To do so, Chinese scholars had to sit gruelling exams consisting of memorized passages from poems and histories. But a pass-mark only lasted for a limited period. They had to resit their exams regularly or they lost their qualifications.

Chinese society had a rigid hierarchy, with the emperor at the top and the common peasants at the bottom. Much of what remains of ancient China concerns the life of the rich and powerful, as only their artefacts have stood the test of time. Since the ancient Chinese invented paper, many of their documents have disintegrated faster than those of less advanced cultures, whose documents were carved in stone or written on parchment. Few buildings remain standing but artefacts found in graves have provided us with evidence of how people lived in ancient China.

CONSULTING THE ORACLE

Since the earliest days of the Shang Dynasty (1600–1100 BC), those who could afford divine guidance sought it from a soothsayer. A hot pointer was pressed against the underpart of a tortoise shell while questions were asked. The cracks that formed were interpreted and the answers etched into the shell as a permanent record.

DECLINING NOBILITY

There were five ranks in ancient Chinese nobility, the Gong, Hou, Bo, Zi and Nan, roughly equivalent to duke, marquis, earl, viscount, and baron. Chinese peerages were hereditary but declined over time. If a family did nothing to justify their honour, each successive generation would fall one rank, until the great-great-great grandson of the original nobleman became a humble commoner. However, the heir of Confucius (see page 28) always kept the highest rank.

A RICH MAN'S HOUSE

The layout of a person's house was said to directly affect the occupant's fortune. Those who could afford it would ensure that their house was positioned to avoid evil spirits and ill winds. The presence of other people's bad fortune could bring disaster, and the perfect gentleman's house was said to be in the quiet countryside; city-dwelling was an evil to be avoided.

TOO RICH TO WORK

Long fingernails were a sign of a person who was wealthy enough not to have to do manual work. Many Chinese let at least one fingernail grow long but the very rich would grow all ten. Nail protectors were worn by the Qing Empress Dowager Zi Xi (1835–1908) to protect her long, carefully manicured nails.

THE SEAL OF AUTHORITY

Letters, documents, orders and even paintings were marked with the owner's seal: a stylized representation of their name. Documents were not accepted as authentic without such a mark. Commoners and low-ranking officials would stamp in red, while high-ranking officials used mauve. During times of national mourning, all seals would use blue ink. Modern seals are roughly a centimetre square, but the emperor's official signature was so large it had to be lifted by two people.

MAGIC STONE

Jade was a prized commodity among the rich. Like all stone, it could be broken but never twisted, making it a symbol of honour and constancy. Jade was also rumoured to have magical powers. An extremely difficult stone to shape, it had to be worn into the required form by laborious sanding.

Life for the Poor

Physical labour was a job for the poor and they were forced to become labourers, builders and farmers to support the rich. Taxation was introduced in about 600 BC, and peasants had to support wars by serving in the army or providing materials, food and money. Peasant families relied heavily on those members who could work while dependents, such as old people and children, were a constant burden. But the old were looked after out of respect, and children were reared to share the work. Respect for elders lasted even after death when, in their afterlife, ancestors were believed to offer prayers to help and protect the family. Many peasants did not own their land. They were tenant-serfs of landlords who could punish them for not working hard enough, which meant they had little opportunity to earn extra money to buy land.

OX POWER

Ideally, an ox was used to pull a plough in the rice paddies. Oxen were not always easy to come by, as most animal herds were on the steppes of Outer China, whereas the farms were in Inner China. Some areas had 'ox-lords' who rented out animals, but many peasants were too poor even to rent one, so had to prepare their fields by hand.

LIFE IN THE CITY

It was considered bad feng shui (see pages 14–15) to live too close to others, as fates would become entwined. The country was spacious but less fortunate people had to live in crowded cities, sharing their neighbours' misfortunes. In both town and country, poor families lived together under one roof, often eating, sleeping and living in the same room, and sometimes sharing it with their animals.

HARD LABOUR

Chinese farm life was hard. In May and June each year there was a whirl of activity: planting, harvesting, moving young rice plants into the fields and harvesting silk worms. Between November and February, with little to do, the large summer workforce became hungry mouths to feed. Working barefoot in rice paddies strewn with manure left the coolies (hired workers) prone to diseases. Such hardships led the Chinese to replace 'coolie' with the word for bitterness and strength: kuli.

LAND LUBBERS

Those who were poor and who lived near the sea often became fishermen, a harsh job, with constant risk from pirate attack. Chinese fishermen rarely strayed far from the coast, and usually sailed in pairs for safety. A small Chinese boat is called a sampan, although today big and small boats both tend to be known as junks (from the Malay word, jong: large boat).

Food & Drink

CORMORANT FISHING

Rods and lines were not the only way to catch fish. Lamps on fishing boats lured fish to the surface where trained cormorants scooped them from the water. Each bird had a collar around its neck to prevent it from swallowing its catch. The fisherman forced the bird to spit the fish out, then sent it back into the water for more. Cormorant fishing is still practised today.

China's vast size meant that its different regions were almost like foreign countries. Each had its own very different crops and dishes, and the distinctive styles of cooking still exist today. In south China, Cantonese food was cooked swiftly in hot oil, while farther north in the Yangzi Valley, more time was taken to prepare sweet-and-sour sauces. Unlike other regional cooking, Tibetan, Mongolian and Manchurian cuisines used a lot of dairy products, whereas the coastal province of Fujian specialized in delicate seafood dishes. The distinctive spicy flavours of Sichuan cooking were only possible after the introduction of the Central American chilli in the 16th century AD.

RICE & RICE CULTURE

During the Tang Dynasty (AD 618–907), quick-ripening varieties of rice were introduced from Vietnam. Canals built to aid transport and famine relief around China also brought water to outlying areas. It was lifted into the fields by a chain-and-paddle system operated by a turning crank. These changes, plus the development of new tools, such as the harrow, made rice-growing essential to feeding China's expanding population. But reliance on one food could cause trouble. If the rice crop failed, the famine affected the entire population.

WHEAT & MILLET

The staple food in ancient China was millet, which was ground into a kind of rough flour. Around AD 500 improvements in milling techniques made wheat more popular, and this formed the major ingredient in most noodle dishes.

ALL THE TEA IN CHINA

Tea, or *cha*, was a popular drink among both rich and poor, and was available in many different varieties to suit every taste and pocket. For the familiar red tea, the leaves were roasted. Other kinds, which used different flavourings and processes, could be sampled in a tea-house – a popular meeting place in ancient China. In the local dialect of south China, cha was pronounced *tay*, from which came the English word. All varieties of modern tea are descended from the Chinese original.

CHOPSTICKS

Metal was often in short supply, and so cooks in ancient China would cut up the food before it was brought to the table. The tiny bite-sized morsels were easy to pick up with wooden sticks, or chopsticks. The Chinese word for chopsticks is *kuaizi* (hasteners), because they hasten the food into the mouth. Chopsticks were used with a hand-held bowl so that the user could manipulate the food more easily.

A TASTE OF THE EXOTIC

Many exotic fruits and vegetables were grown in ancient China. They included lychee fruits (see left), longans (dragon's eyes), water-chestnuts, snow-peas, bitter melons and Chinese cabbage (*bak choi*: 'white vegetable'). All of which helped to give Chinese food its distinctive flavour and texture.

Pastimes

BOOK OF CHANGES

The I Ching is an ancient system of fortune-telling. Advice and answers to important personal questions were, and still are, sought by referring to a text, in which a chapter between 1 and 64 is consulted at random by throwing sticks or coins. The picture shows the eight three-line trigrams that are combined with one another to create the 64 numbers.

There were good and bad pastimes according to the Imperial government. Singing the praises of the emperor, watching approved dramas and martial training were all thought to be good ways of strengthening the nation. Excessive drinking, gambling and lewd behaviour were all frowned upon. Plays that ridiculed the ruling dynasty were outlawed.

CHINESE CHESS

Chess was invented in India, but the Chinese had already adopted it by AD 570. Chinese chess is very different to the common version. It is played on a board of 64 squares but the pieces move along the lines between them, and the kings cannot leave their four-square palaces. The 32 pieces are all the same size and shape, each one inscribed with its functions. As well as horses, chariots, ministers and soldiers, the Chinese chessboard has elephants, guardsmen and cannons.

CHINESE OPERA

Performances of music and song, popular since the 7th century AD, eventually developed into Chinese opera. All the actors had to be male. They were divided into four classes of character, known as Sheng (emperors, generals, gentlemen), Qing (villains, rebels, outlaws), Dan (female roles) and Chou (comic relief).

READING THE FUTURE

Ancient China had its own unique systems for telling fortunes, including face reading, which looked at marks and lines on the face, and the I Ching. Other systems developed over time and palm readers and astrologers could often be found telling fortunes on the streets.

BOOK OF SONGS

In order to report the mood of the people to the emperor, a government agency called the *Yue-fu* was established in 120 BC. Its officials regularly travelled through the countryside writing down the songs they heard. These reports survive as the Book of Songs – perhaps the oldest pop charts in the world. Some of the earliest Chinese instruments included stone chimes, bamboo flutes, the *pipa* (lute), *huiqin* (fiddle) and *qin* (zither), all of which are illustrated here.

HIGH-FLYING

As early as the 2nd century BC, kites were used for military signalling in China. Physicians recommended kite-flying as an activity for young boys to make them throw back their heads and open their mouths, thereby cooling the body's energy levels. Early kites were shaped like a kite, the bird from which they were named, but later developments included dragon-shapes (that fought to cut each other's tails), kites that could carry a human scout, and exploding kites that carried firecrackers on their strings. This modern kite looks like a space-age version of a coiled dragon.

PUPPET MASTERS

Puppetry originated in China and is still a common form of entertainment throughout Asia. But not just an entertainment, puppetry once saved an emperor's life. In 206 BC, giant puppets were moved around on the walls of a city in order to convince the besieging rebels that Emperor Gao Zi was still within. By the time the ruse was discovered, he had already made his getaway.

Fashion

Common people in ancient China mainly wore clothes made of hemp or ramie-grass. In the 14th century AD, they began growing cotton brought in from South Asia, which was found to be warmer and more profitable to grow. Clothes were not just items to keep the body warm. They were important indicators of status, and high-ranking officials had to take great care with their appearance. Chinese clothes were often decorated with mythical animals to protect the wearer from harm and bring them good fortune.

Most dragons were drawn with three or four claws on each limb. Five-clawed dragons were reserved for the Imperial family.

KEEPING COOL

Early fans were flat, rigid panels used by both men and women to keep cool. The folding variety was invented in Japan in the 4th century AD, and eagerly adopted by the Chinese before the 11th century. It was important among the rich to have the right fan for the right season, and writing or painting on someone's fan was a sign of friendship. A deserted wife was called an 'autumn fan'.

THE SILK MYSTERY

Silk was one of China's most important commodities, and has been manufactured for well over 2,000 years. The silk road was the lengthy trade route between Asia and Europe, where Chinese silk was prized as early as Roman times. A light, soft fabric with a shimmering quality, silk was in great demand abroad, and foreign powers were desperate to know the secret of its manufacture. In the 6th century AD, European spies managed to discover the incredible truth: it was made from a delicate gossamer thread unwound from the cocoons of silkworm moths.

MEN OF THE CLOTH

Mandarins and other officials had to wear elaborate clothing and jewels to show their rank. But monks and priests took a vow of poverty and wore very simple, humble robes.

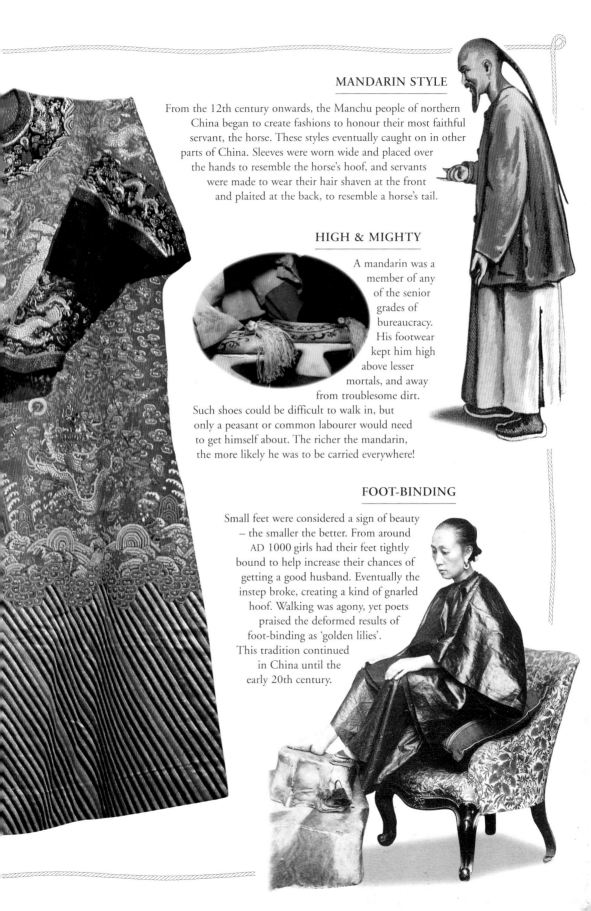

MANDARIN STYLE

From the 12th century onwards, the Manchu people of northern China began to create fashions to honour their most faithful servant, the horse. These styles eventually caught on in other parts of China. Sleeves were worn wide and placed over the hands to resemble the horse's hoof, and servants were made to wear their hair shaven at the front and plaited at the back, to resemble a horse's tail.

HIGH & MIGHTY

A mandarin was a member of any of the senior grades of bureaucracy. His footwear kept him high above lesser mortals, and away from troublesome dirt. Such shoes could be difficult to walk in, but only a peasant or common labourer would need to get himself about. The richer the mandarin, the more likely he was to be carried everywhere!

FOOT-BINDING

Small feet were considered a sign of beauty – the smaller the better. From around AD 1000 girls had their feet tightly bound to help increase their chances of getting a good husband. Eventually the instep broke, creating a kind of gnarled hoof. Walking was agony, yet poets praised the deformed results of foot-binding as 'golden lilies'. This tradition continued in China until the early 20th century.

Art & Architecture

FINE FIGURES

Sculpture was highly-regarded from early times. This white earthenware horse was found in the grave of Zhang Shigui, a nobleman from the Tang Dynasty (AD 618–907).

The wealth and sophistication of ancient China created some of the most valuable treasures in the world. In times when the empire was strong and stable, such as at the height of the Song and Tang Dynasties, Chinese arts flourished in every conceivable medium, including bronze statuary, silken textiles, lacquer work, ink paintings and decorated porcelain. Chinese architecture avoided hard edges and corners in favour of soft curves as seen in the wing-like shape of Chinese roofs. It was believed that this softer style created good *qi* (energy). A similar emphasis on flowing shapes and natural harmony is found in the other arts. Chinese painters often concentrated on landscape scenes of *shan shui* (mountains and water), with swirling mists and tiny human figures dwarfed by the beauty of nature.

FENG SHUI

Feng shui (wind and water) is that which can be felt but not seen, grasped but not held. Originally used to find auspicious sites for graves in the 3rd century AD, this set of beliefs and superstitions was adapted to help the living counter unlucky influences in their homes. Even today, feng shui masters use a complex compass, such as this one, to determine the lucky and unlucky influences caused by the position of a house.

BRONZE-AGE ART

The Shang people flourished in north China around 1000 BC, and were incredibly advanced forgers of bronze ware, which they decorated with images of mythical-monster masks and animal figures. Some pictures were broken up into square thunder-pattern spirals, or leiwen, with just an eye remaining to indicate it symbolized a living creature.

THE FORBIDDEN CITY

The capital city of China, Beijing, was designed along regular, square, grid patterns, which were good for transport. The north–south and east–west alignment of the square deliberately evoked the feng shui of ancient times. In 1420 a walled citadel was built in the middle as a home for the emperor and his family. Closed to outsiders, it was known as the Forbidden City.

Health & Medicine

Chinese medicine is based on herbal cures and the theory of qi – an energy believed to be in all living things. A person's qi had to be kept healthy and balanced, otherwise they would fall ill. Qi was maintained through eating a healthy diet and getting sufficient exercise. However, while the ancient Chinese had medical beliefs, they lacked medical science. Some cures worked by accident, while others did more harm than good. No system was in place to prove those cures that worked and those that didn't. Matters were not helped by shyness; doctors could not touch female patients, and instead had to use a doll to indicate where the pain was.

MOXIBUSTION

Some aches and pains were treated with moxibustion, which involved making pastilles from the dried leaves of the moxa plant, applying them to the skin and setting them on fire (normally under a glass to contain the heat). This practice is still in use today.

MAN ROOT

Ginseng, which became widespread after the 12th century AD, is an aromatic root, often shaped like a man and highly prized for its medicinal properties. All ginseng in China was considered the property of the emperor, though he would often bestow quantities of it upon his loyal subjects. It was believed that the ginseng plant would turn into a white-blooded man if left undisturbed for 300 years and that the blood of such a man could raise the dead.

ACUPUNCTURE

The Chinese believed that energy circulates throughout the body but could be unbalanced if the channels became blocked. In the 1st century AD, the science of acupuncture was devised to treat this problem. It involved sticking needles into the body at special points as shown on this statue. Still in use today, it is thought to stimulate the body's own defence mechanisms, and is also used as an anaesthetic.

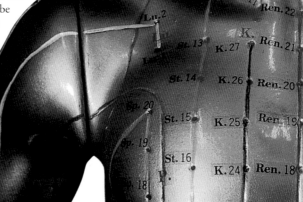

OPIUM WARS

Opium was widely used in China as a painkiller, but was put to other uses during the late Ming Dynasty (1368–1644). With the arrival of tobacco from America, people began to smoke a mixture of the two drugs. Listless, weak opium addicts became a major problem, and the drug was banned. However, large quantities arrived with British traders, who used it to pay for tea. In 1840, this led to the Opium War which ended with China defeated and Britain occupying Hong Kong as part of the settlement.

MORNING EXERCISE

The Chinese have always believed that exercise and clean living strengthens the body's energy and extends the natural lifespan. One such exercise was *tai qi*, a combined regime of callisthenics that could also be used as a martial art. Strengthening the body, it was said, would also strengthen the mind. Other physical exercises included gong fu boxing, which we know today as kung fu.

MYSTERY CURES

The lack of scientific method in Chinese medicine has meant that some cures work well, whereas others are merely based on superstition. Deer horns were imported in vast quantities for use in medicines, most probably because the word in Chinese for deer sounds a little like 'ease' in some dialects.

Love & Marriage

In ancient China people were expected to put their family duty ahead of their personal feelings. Marriages were arranged by professional matchmakers, sometimes before the bride and groom were even born. Such alliances turned enemies into in-laws who were then obliged to respect and help each other. A bride had to leave her family behind and become a member of her husband's family. In her new home, she would have to worship his ancestors and obey his parents.

LOVE BIRDS

Because mandarin ducks mate for life they have become the Chinese symbol of a loving and faithful marriage. Wild geese in flight were the symbols of communication from afar. They crop up in many poems about lovers forced to live apart, waiting for news of each other.

SECOND-CLASS WIVES

A man could have only one wife who would share any title or honours he gained during his life. However, he was free to take concubines to increase his chances of having more children. As a second-rank 'wife', a concubine was liable to be badly treated by both her 'husband's' mother and his first wife.

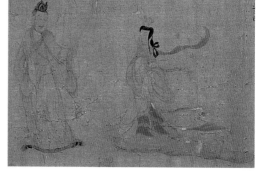

DIVORCE

A man could divorce his wife if she was barren, lascivious or jealous, or if she had a disease, stole anything or neglected to honour her in-laws. She could even be divorced if she talked too much. However, he could not divorce her during a period of mourning, if he had come into money or if she had no home to return to.

FATAL ATTRACTION

The most beautiful woman in Chinese history was said to be Yang Guifei, an 8th century companion of Emperor Xuanzong. He was so infatuated with her that he neglected his kingdom and appointed members of her family to high offices. The last straw came when he made her cousin prime minister. There was a rebellion and she was killed.

MARRIAGE RITUALS

Before a marriage took place, the year, month, day and hour of the bride and groom's birth were checked to ensure that the union would bring good fortune. On the chosen (lucky) day, the bride wore red and was taken to the groom's home in a sedan chair. The pair worshipped the groom's ancestors together, leaving the shrine as man and wife. Until the beginning of the Sui Dynasty (AD 581), Chinese women had to wear veils when they went outside the house. This custom is still practised at many Chinese weddings today.

LU'S LOVE LOST

The Zhinan temple complex in Taiwan is sacred to Lu Dongbin, one of the eight Immortals of Chinese legend, who was thwarted in love. It is unlucky for lovers to visit the temple together, lest they be parted by the Immortal's jealous anger.

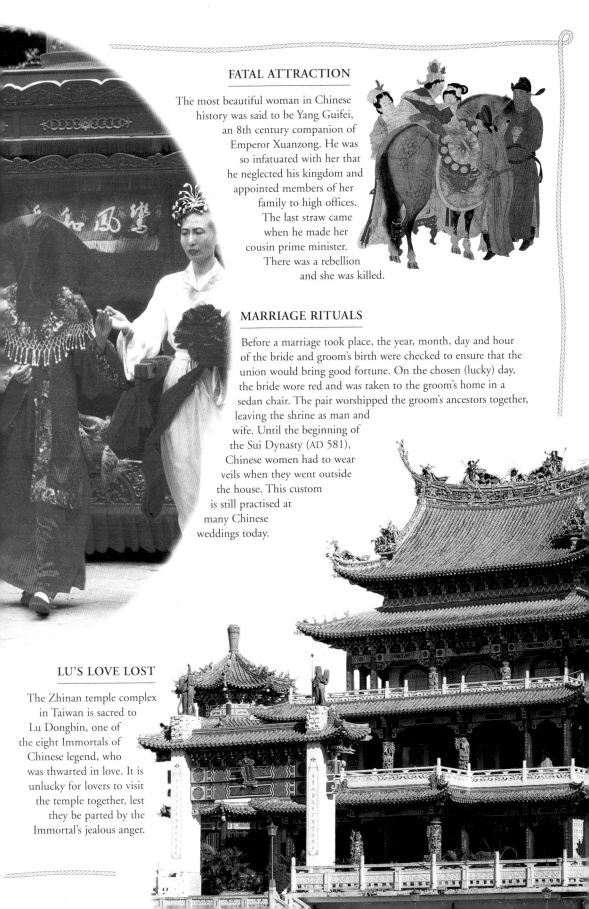

Women & Children

According to ancient Chinese philosophy the universe was a place in constant search of harmony and balance. As applied to men and women it was considered the man's duty to command and the woman's duty to obey. Real life, however, wasn't so simple. Women could exert great authority over their children, and several emperors were puppets of their powerful mothers. Though sworn to obey her husband, a wife was the boss at home. Even the philosopher Confucius once complained: *'When she's close, she's insolent. When she's far away, she nags.'*

POMEGRANATE

A pomegranate is a fruit bursting with seeds, and so became a Chinese symbol of fertility. Pomegranates were placed in the homes of couples who hoped to have more children. However, couples who already had too many mouths to feed tried to avoid them at all costs.

THE EMPRESS DOWAGER

The Empress Dowager Zi Xi (1835–1908) was the last of many female rulers, stretching back to the 1st century AD, who put a weakling on the throne so she could rule from behind the scenes. The weakling in question was her own son, the Tongzhi Emperor. Although an emperor was all-powerful, he was still obliged to obey his surviving parents, and sometimes a mother could use her power over her son to rule the whole nation.

UNICORN FATE

The Chinese unicorn, or *jilin*, was said to have appeared shortly before the death of Confucius, and to herald a time of great peace and prosperity. A unicorn is thought to bring luck to parents in the form of a genius child, and images of them were often kept near cradles. Such legends of fantastical creatures were reinforced when Admiral Zheng-He brought back a giraffe from his sea journey to Africa, and astounded the Chinese court.

CELESTIAL BIRDS

As the dragon was the symbol of the male, the phoenix was the symbol of the female. Phoenix designs can be found on many articles of female clothing and jewellery throughout Chinese history.

CHILDREN

Children were expected to work from a very young age. Peasant sons worked in the fields with their parents. As young as seven, children were given adult tasks and responsibilities. Chinese ages were counted from one, not zero, so children were one year old the moment they were born. Instead of having birthdays, everyone would add a year to their age at each Chinese New Year, so it was technically possible for a child born on New Year's Eve to be two years old the following morning.

SILK SPINNING

While their brothers were in the fields, girls had to spin and weave. A poor family dreaded the birth of a girl. She would be one more mouth to feed until they could marry her off, at which point they would have to pay a dowry to her prospective husband's family. Whatever happened, the bride rarely had much say in her fate. According to Confucian tradition, a girl was supposed to obey her parents until she married, her husband until his death and her eldest son until her own death.

ALIEN INVADERS

The Great Wall didn't always work. In the 4th century AD, it was crossed by the Tabgatch people of Inner Mongolia, who founded the Wei Dynasty. In the 12th century, the people of the steppes were united under their strongest ruler ever, Genghis Khan. His grandson Kublai conquered China and founded the Yuan Dynasty in 1271. It was breached for the last time in the 17th century, when the Manchus invaded and stayed to rule China right up until the early 20th century.

ARMOUR

Robes restricted movement, so Chinese soldiers wore trousers to make horse-riding easier. Tough leather protected most parts of the body, with extra quilting to reduce the impact of blows. Cavalrymen wore extra leg protection. Metal plates were uncommon, except on the chest in later years. Most soldiers had small metal studs to deflect enemy blades. Chinese soldiers often painted a tiger's head on their shields, or even wore imitation tiger-skins, complete with a fake tail. As 'King of Beasts', an image of the tiger was meant to strike fear into the hearts of China's enemies.

CLAY SOLDIERS

We know a great deal about Chinese warfare from the evidence found at archaeological sites, especially the Qin Emperor's famous Terracotta Army. It consisted of over 6,000 lifelike statues guarding his tomb. Most of the soldiers, however, are empty-handed. The real weapons they had carried were looted during a rebellion in 206 BC.

War & Weaponry

In some parts of China the climate will support only farming; in others, only herding. The northern border zone supports both, and so throughout history, it has been fought over constantly. The greatest threats to China came from the plains of Asia, from horse-riding tribes such as the Mongols and the Xiong-nu (Huns). China's soldiers had advanced weaponry to fight off the barbarian (foreign) invaders. Iron weapons replaced inferior bronze during the 7th century BC, around the time that the Chinese invented the crossbow. From 500 BC, horses were ridden instead of simply being used to pull chariots. Triple ranks of archers and crossbowmen kept up a continuous rain of arrows, charioteers and horsemen charged through enemy ranks, and humble footsoldiers attacked with swords and spears.

FIRE POWDER

Gunpowder was first used in fireworks during the 7th century AD. Today, firecrackers are still used to scare off evil spirits at important occasions. Some were also used for military purposes, fired into enemy ranks to cause chaos. Actual guns of Western origin were first used in China by Mongol invaders under Genghis and Kublai Khan.

GREAT WALL

The First Emperor ordered the Great Wall of China to be built as a defence against invasion by the nomadic tribes of the plains beyond China. Overall, it was about 6,000 km (4,000 miles) long and had a series of watchtowers along its length. Although parts of it date from the 3rd century BC, the most famous views we see are those restored in the Ming Dynasty during the 15th and 16th centuries. At its western end, it is little more than a bank of mud.

POMP & CEREMONY

Not all weapons were for warfare. This Shang Dynasty axe has a bronze handle and a blade of jade which would not have been much use in battle. More likely, it was used for ceremonial purposes. A jade blade was believed to have magical properties.

Crime & Punishment

Chinese judges would have had images of cranes in their courtrooms, and the bird eventually became a symbol of justice itself.

Several types of punishment were used against wrong-doers in ancient China. The mildest were flogging or being locked into wooden stocks. The next level involved banishment, either for a limited period or permanently. A death sentence also varied with the severity of the crime. The simplest method was a straightforward beheading, but truly evil criminals (such as those who had murdered their parents) were treated to the terrible 'lingering death', by which they were slowly cut to pieces whilst still alive.

STREET WISE

Strict rules governed the right-of-way on Chinese streets. Pedestrians had to make way for coolies carrying heavy loads. Coolies had to make way for empty sedan chairs. Empty sedan chairs had to make way for occupied sedans. Chairs had to make way for horses, and *everyone* had to make way for a wedding procession or an important official. Because it was polite to dismount to greet friends, pedestrians often used a fan to hide their face from acquaintances who were on horseback or in a sedan chair. Otherwise, the friend would be obliged to get down to say hello.

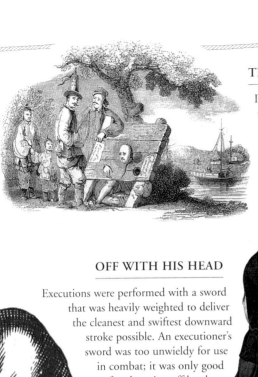

THE CRIMINAL'S YOKE

Petty thieves and other minor criminals were forced to wear a heavy wooden collar called a *cangue*. It was generally taken off at night but during the day they would have to rely on their friends for help, as they couldn't feed themselves.

OFF WITH HIS HEAD

Executions were performed with a sword that was heavily weighted to deliver the cleanest and swiftest downward stroke possible. An executioner's sword was too unwieldy for use in combat; it was only good for chopping off heads.

CANING

Some criminals were flogged with a lash made from a strip of bamboo that had been planed smooth. There were two kinds of instrument, the heavy and the light, and the criminal would be struck across the back. However, Emperor Kang Xi of the Qing Dynasty decreed that beating the buttocks was preferable, as there was less risk of damaging internal organs.

METHODS OF TORTURE

Magistrates were allowed to use torture to extract confessions. Men were flogged, and women could be slapped on the cheeks with a piece of leather. Chinese water torture involved the slow dripping of water onto the victim, who was usually wrapped in a cloth. As it slowly became soaked it made it almost impossible for the person to breathe. There was also a device for squeezing the fingers or the ankles until the bones rubbed together painfully.

WHEELBARROWS

The earliest plans for the Chinese wheelbarrow date back to the 1st century AD. With the wheel under the main part, it could easily lift 135 kg (300 lb) of weight, and was used extensively to replace a cart on narrow tracks.

WATER CLOCKS

Time was kept with a clepsydra or water clock, which originally consisted of several jars. They each emptied after a set time, and more exact measurements could be made with a bamboo dipstick to see how much water (and time) was remaining. Water clocks are a very old invention in China, but were not mentioned in literature earlier than the 1st century BC.

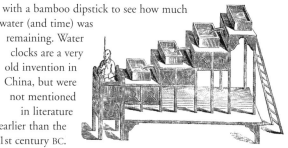

PAPER, PULP & PARCHMENT

Though a form of parchment was in use in China during the Han Dynasty, the legendary inventor of paper was Cai Lun, who died in AD 114. He is said to have made his first sheets from old linen, tow, and pieces of fishnet. Paper made from rice straw or bamboo pulp was used in the normal way. Stronger papyrus sheets were used in windows as a cheap alternative to glass. It was considered extremely bad luck to step on paper inscribed with words, or even to throw it away. It had to be carefully burned to avoid ill fortune. This picture shows the fresh wet paper being laid out on racks to dry in the sun.

THE BURNING OF THE BOOKS

In 213 BC, the Qin Emperor, on advice from his prime minister, decided to burn all records of previous dynasties and all books that were not for soothsaying or of medical or agricultural use. The Qin Dynasty was believed to be so great that no previous literature could be of interest. Important and irreplaceable documents and records of discoveries were burnt. This also helped the Qin Emperor control what the population read. Hundreds of people were burned alive when they were found to be hiding books. Books from before this period have only survived by accident. Several hundred years later, in the Liang Dynasty, Emperor Yuan burned another 140,000 books for similar reasons.

Transport & Science

Despite occasional disasters, such as the Burning of the Books, the Chinese were an advanced civilization. In warfare they had crossbows and fireworks, and in industry they were using water wheels to power bellows in forges as early as the 1st century AD. But 'science', as a method of improving earlier ideas, was almost unknown. In later centuries, China was limited by its own education system. Even in the 19th century, the only way to get ahead was by studying the classics, and officials frowned upon people with knowledge of new-fangled arts like engineering, steam trains or medicine.

COUNTING BOARDS

Mathematics in China was done with an abacus, or counting board, often said to be a primitive form of computer. Each row represents units, tens, hundreds, thousands and so on, and calculation can be as fast as with a pen and paper. But, with pen and paper it's possible to check back for mistakes. Our word abacus comes from the Hebrew for dust on a tabletop (abak), in which people wrote their sums.

CATCHING QUAKES

The scientist Zhang Heng invented this earthquake detector in AD 132. An internal pendulum would knock against the sides if there was a tremor, causing a ball to fall from a dragon's mouth into a frog's mouth. Exactly which frog caught which ball would show the direction of the quake. A year before his death in AD 138, Zhang used the device to detect an earthquake 373 miles away.

SEDAN CHAIRS

Important officials would be carried by a team of men in a sedan chair. The emperor was allowed sixteen bearers, princes and governors had eight and other officials had four. Others who could afford it were only permitted two.

DAOISM

Daoism was founded in the 6th century BC by Lao Zi. It was a philosophy that preached harmony in all things, represented by the uniting of chaos and law, negative and positive and earth and sky in the yin-yang symbol.

Religion

In ancient China, it was considered rude to impose upon those who were too high above or far below oneself in rank, and this even applied in the afterlife. Worshippers could only pray to their ancestors and family, or spirits of a similar class. The Chinese believed that the next world was very like our own, and that they could send aid to their ancestors by burning paper effigies in the real world. The emperor prayed to the most powerful gods, to keep the land free of flood and famine. Natural disasters were sometimes used as excuses for revolts, blamed on an emperor who was failing in his divine duties. As in China today, there was no single religion, but several belief systems which existed side-by-side.

CONFUCIANISM

Confucius sought to make the world a better place with precise rules on a small scale. He thought that if each person knew their place in the family, then each village, city and province would be strengthened, and ultimately the entire state would become perfect. Confucianism preached loyalty and respect to the ancestors.

BUDDHISM

Buddhism first arrived in China from India in the 1st century AD, though there are earlier stories about Buddhist missionaries imprisoned by the Qin Emperor and rescued by an angel. Initially an urban religion, it slowly spread into the countryside as believers mixed it with elements of Daoism. Buddhists believe that you can only be truly happy when you stop wanting things and work to remove all desire from your life. Their ultimate aim is to achieve enlightenment through reincarnation.

BURNING INCENSE

Incense is made from the dust of certain sweet-smelling woods, mixed with clay. The sticks then burn slowly to fill the air with their perfume; some were even marked to show the passing of time. In ancient China, incense was burned as a way of honouring the gods.

HOROSCOPES

Chinese horoscopes were an important part of everyday life. Fortune-tellers would ascertain which of twelve different animals ruled the year of someone's birth. The animals were the Rat, Ox, Tiger, Rabbit, Dragon, Snake, Horse, Sheep, Monkey, Rooster, Dog and Pig, at which time the cycle would return to the Rat. The year 2000 was ruled by the Dragon, so you can count forward or backward to work out which animal rules you.

FOREIGN FAITHS

Buddhism is not the only foreign import. Many of China's ethnic groups have their own beliefs, including thousand-year-old communities of Christians and Muslims. This is the Potala palace, the former home of the religious leader of Tibet, the Dalai Lama.

EVIL SPIRITS

The magical art of feng shui sought to protect the living from predatory ghosts and evil spirits. It was believed that symbolic guardians could keep supernatural threats at bay, hence statues like this fearsome stone lion, found outside a Chinese tomb.

Legacy of the Past

GOOD MEDICINE

The positive aspects of Chinese medicine, such as herbalism and acupuncture, have spread throughout the world. Today, it is rare for a city to be without at least one shop selling traditional Chinese remedies.

The greatest legacy of ancient China is modern China. Unlike many other past civilizations, it is still with us today, bigger and more powerful than before. But there are many different Chinas. There is the ancient historical civilization, the vast Communist state, the 'little dragon' Chinese nations like Singapore and Taiwan and the millions of people all around the world who are ethnic Chinese. There are no emperors any more, but China is still a great superpower and central in world politics and trade. The people still call their nation Zhong Guo, 'the Middle Kingdom'.

HONG KONG

Taken by the British after the Opium War, Hong Kong was returned to China in 1997. In the interim, it had grown into a centre of commerce, the tiny area of land turning into a forest of skyscrapers. This giant building is owned by the Bank of China, and was designed in accordance with the rules of feng shui. Some locals disagreed, suggesting that it looked like a giant dagger: very bad luck.

THE BALLAD OF MULAN

In the 6th century AD, songs were sung about Hua Mulan ('Magnolia Flower'), a girl who joined the army in her father's place. She fought for 12 years disguised as a man, but when she was offered a place in the Khan's court (China at the time was ruled by foreign Tabgatch nomads), she begged instead to be given a camel on which she could ride home to her family. The story is still famous today.

FISTS OF FURY

Bruce Lee (1940-1973) is still one of the most well-known Chinese faces around the world. Born in the United States, Lee became a martial arts teacher on the west coast of America. He is best remembered for his kung fu films such as *Enter the Dragon*. Lee and his successors popularized Chinese martial arts as a sport abroad.

THE EAST IS RED

The Last Emperor was overthrown in 1912, but the Republic of China soon had difficulties. After Japanese invasion and a civil war, the Republicans were forced to retreat to the island of Taiwan and Chairman Mao, a former librarian, proclaimed the People's Republic in 1949. Though the Communists were unquestionably the masters of China, the Republicans in Taiwan still claimed to be the true rulers. The United States did not recognize the Communists until 1973, when President Nixon went on a goodwill visit.

DID YOU KNOW?

There are thousands of Chinese characters? The total number of Chinese characters and variants is estimated at 40,000, though nobody could possibly list or learn them all. The majority are ancient, extinct words or extremely complex ideas in specialist fields. To reach a reasonable level of Chinese reading ability, you would need to memorize a much smaller number: maybe just 5,000.

That martial artists once fought a war against Christians? Christianity took root in parts of China from AD 631. When organized bands of missionaries arrived many centuries later, the locals were heard to complain that the sharp church spires erected by the 'Jesus devils' upset the area's feng shui. Towards the close of the Qing dynasty in 1899, poor areas saw the Boxer Uprising against Christianity and all other foreign influences. The Boxers were martial artists who claimed to have a magic invulnerability to foreign blades and bullets. Some would enter trances to be possessed by the God of War.

That goldfish are baby dragons? According to some Chinese tales, a goldfish turns into a dragon when it dies and passes through the Gates of Heaven. It will return to wreak vengeance if owners have mistreated it, or grant them great fortune if they were kind to it.

Gold and silk can kill? In ancient Chinese records, if someone was said to have 'swallowed gold' it meant they drank poison and killed themselves. If an official was 'presented with silk', it was a command from the emperor that they should be strangled.

Midnight guessing games were banned? Chai Mui is a game played by two people holding up a hand each, with some, all or none of the fingers displayed, and simultaneously shouting out a guess at the sum of the two hands. The closest guess was the winner. During the Qing dynasty, games of Chai Mui became so loud that the Governor of Hong Kong banned them between 11pm and 6am.

PRONUNCIATION

**Most of the Chinese words in this book sound as they look to you.
The following letters are pronounced differently:**

c = ts, I = ee after all consonants except c, ch, s, z, and zh, when it sounds like yrrh.

q = ch, x = hs (pronounced fast) **z = dz, zh = j**

ACKNOWLEDGEMENTS

For Ellis Tinios

We would like to thank: Helen Wire, David Hobbs and Elizabeth Wiggans

Copyright © 2000 ticktock Publishing Ltd.

First published in Great Britain by ticktock Publishing Ltd., The Offices in the Square, Hadlow, Tonbridge, Kent, TN11 0DD. All rights reserved.

No part of this publication may be reproduced, stored in a retrieval system, or transmitted in any form or by any means electronic, mechanical, photocopying, recording or otherwise, without prior written permission of the copyright owner.

A CIP catalogue record for this book is available from the British Library. ISBN 1 86007 159 7 (paperback). ISBN 1 86007 226 7 (hardback).

Picture research by Image Select. Printed in Spain.

Picture Credits:

t=top, b=bottom, c=centre, l=left, r=right, OFC=outside front cover, IFC=inside front cover, IBC=inside back cover, OBC=outside back cover

AKG Photos; 4bl, 4tl, 5tl, 9t,9br, 11tr, 11cl, 13br, 16bl, 17t, 24cr, 25tr, 26tr & OBC bc, 26/27c, 27bl, 28/29c, OFC (main pic) & OFCcr. Ancient Art & Architecture Collection; 2tl, 2bl, 3br, 4cb, 12bl, 21tr, 21bl, 25tl, 27tr, 29cl, 29tr. The British Museum; 18br. Ann Ronan @ Image Select; 2/3c, 6tr, 6/7, 13tr & OBC cr, 14/15, 20cr, 20/21cr, 28bl, 32c. Corbis; 4c, 10cl, 12fl, 13cl, 17br, 20tl, 25br, e.t. archive; 8cr, 19tr, 22tl, OFCtr, OFCtc & OFCbr. Heather Angel; 16tl. Holt Studios International; 8bl, 9bl. The Hutchinson Library; 18/19c. Images Colour Library; 10tl, 14/15tr, 16/17c. Image Select; 6bl, 6br, 22bl, 23bl, 26bl, 29tl, 30br, 31bl. Jean Loup Charmet; 26c. Oxford Scientific Films; 18tl, 24tl. Ronald Grant Archive; 30bl, 31. Science & Society; 27br. Spectrum; 10/11c & IFC, 11cr, 17cl, 19br, 23tr. Still Pictures; 30tr. Tony Stone Images; 8tl & OBCtr, 22cr. Werner Foreman Archive; 5tr, 11br, 12/13c, 20bl, 23b, 29br. 24/25c *Everyday Life through the Ages* by Reader's Digest.

Every effort has been made to trace the copyright holders and we apologize in advance for any unintentional omissions. We would be pleased to insert the appropriate acknowledgement in any subsequent edition of this publication.

**snapping-turtle
guide**